PRESENTED TO

_____

FROM

_____

DATE

Poems for Mother

LOVING THOUGHTS

IDEALS PUBLICATIONS INCORPORATED
NASHVILLE, TENNESSEE

ISBN 0-8249-4175-6

Printed and bound by R. R. Donnelly & Sons in Mexico.

Published by Ideals Publications Incorporated
535 Metroplex Drive, Suite 250
Nashville, Tennessee 37211

Library of Congress Cataloging-in-Publication Data
Poems for mother: loving thoughts / Thorunn McCoy
    p.cm.
  ISBN 0-8249-4175-6 (alk. paper)
   1. Mothers--Poetry. 2. Motherhood--Poetry. 3. American Poetry--
20th century. 4. Mothers--Quotations, maxims, etc. 5. Motherhood--
Quotations, maxims, etc. I. McCoy, Thorunn, 1968-
PS595.M64 P63 1999
811.008'03520431--dc21   99-058500

10 8 6 4 2 1 3 5 7 9

THORUNN RUGA MCCOY, EDITOR
EVE DEGRIE, DESIGNER
ELIZABETH BONNER KEA, COPY EDITOR

ACKNOWLEDGMENTS

Ideals Publications Incorporated has made every effort to trace the ownership of all copyrighted material. Thanks are due to the following authors, publishers, and agents for permission to use the material indicated: CLIFTON, LUCILLE. "my mama moved among the days" copyright © 1987 by Lucille Clifton. Reprinted from GOOD WOMAN: POEMS AND A MEMOIR 1969-1980, by Lucille Clifton, with permission of BOA Editions, Ltd. CUMMINGS, E. E. "if there are any heavens my mother will(all by herself)have", copyright 1931, © 1959, 1991 by the Trustees for the E. E. Cummings Trust. Copyright © 1979 by George James Firmage, from COMPLETE POEMS: 1904-1962 by E. E. Cummings, Edited by George J. Firmage. Reprinted by permission of Liveright Publishing Corporation. GUEST , EDGAR. "Mother's Day" from LIVING THE YEARS by Edgar Guest. Reprinted by permission of Henry Sobell, Jr. JONES, RODNEY. "Caught", from TRANSPARENT GESTURES. Copyright © 1989 by Rodney Jones. Reprinted by permission of Houghton Mifflin Company. All rights reserved. *Acknowledgments continue on page 88.*

TO MY MOTHER

You too, my mother, read my rhymes
For love of unforgotten times,
And you may chance to hear once more
The little feet along the floor.

—ROBERT LOUIS STEVENSON

There is nothing sweeter than the heart of a pious mother. —MARTIN LUTHER

THE MOTHER'S HYMN

Lord, who ordainest for mankind
Benignant toils and tender cares,
We thank Thee for the ties that bind
The mother to the child she bears.

We thank Thee for the hopes that rise
Within her heart as, day by day,
The dawning soul, from those young eyes,
Looks with a clearer, steadier ray.

And grateful for the blessing given
With that dear infant on her knee,
She trains the eye to look to heaven,
The voice to lisp a prayer to Thee.

Such thanks the blessed Mary gave
When from her lap the holy Child,
Sent from on high to seek and save
The lost of earth, looked up and smiled.

All-Gracious! Grant to those who bear
A mother's charge the strength and light
To guide the feet that own their care
In ways of love and truth and right.

—WILLIAM CULLEN BRYANT

Home to me is Mother; home to me is love. —MARY LOBERG

MOTHER OF MINE

Mother in gladness, Mother in sorrow,
Mother today, and Mother tomorrow,
With arms ever open to fold and caress you,
O Mother of Mine, may God keep you and bless you.

—W. DAYTON WEDGEFARTH

FAITH

We children turned to Mother
For her approving nod—
As sure of understanding
As when mother turned to God.

—VIRGINIA SCOTT MINER

For unwearying patience and unchanging tenderness, the love of a true mother stands next to the love of our Father in heaven.

—AUTHOR UNKNOWN

Into a woman's keeping is committed the destiny of the generations to come after us. —THEODORE ROOSEVELT

She is the guardian angel of the family, the queen, the tender hand of love. A mother is the best friend anyone ever has. A mother is love.

—AUTHOR UNKNOWN

THE OLD, DEAR RIGHT

As years ago we carried to your knees
The tales and treasures of eventful days,
Knowing no deed too humble for your praise,
Nor any gift too trivial to please,
So still we bring, with older smiles and tears,
What gifts we may, to claim the old, dear right;
Your faith, beyond the silence and the night,
Your love still close and watching through the years.

—KATHLEEN NORRIS

YOUR GIFTS

You could not give me toys in those bleak days;
So when my playmates proudly boasted theirs,
You caught me to the shelter of your arms,
And taught me how to laugh away my tears.
Having no books, you sang a shining word
Into my open palm and closed it tight,
And some far god of little children heard,
And gave you of his best for my delight.

So when the neighbors' children shouted by,
Their hired nursemaids herding them like sheep;
Then, that old dauntless look of yours would leap,
And, leading me beneath the western skies,
You woke their mirrored glory in my eyes.

And there were nights; do you remember still?
Forgetting playthings we could never buy,
We journeyed out beyond the farthest hill,
Adventuring along the evening sky;
And you would teach the meaning of the stars.
Not the dull purpose vaguely guessed by sages
And catalogued in musty study-books,
But wild, fantastic legends of lost ages,
That none but their creator ever knew,
And that he whispered only once to one
Frail, lonely mother—and that mother—you.
—DUBOSE HEYWARD

*B*eing a mother enables one to influence the future.
—JANE SELLMAN

MOTHERS

In a mother undefiled
Prayer goeth on in sleep, as true
And pauseless as the pulses do.
—ELIZABETH BARRETT BROWNING

With gentle hands God made the flowers,
Fashioning them with care.
He brushed the sky with pink and gold,
Leaving a sunset there;
Beautified the earth with trees—
These works and countless others;
But for His greatest masterpiece,
God created mothers.
—LELA BERNARD

The pondering of a mother, if it could be written—if there were an angelic reportorial hand to take the best thoughts and the sweetest fancies, and the life of a mother's heart could be written in those early brooding days, it would shine fit to be read in the libraries of the heavenly world itself. —CATHERINE BEECHER

THIRTEEN

ONLY ONE MOTHER

Hundreds of stars in the pretty sky,
    Hundreds of shells on the shore together,
    Hundreds of birds that go singing by,
    Hundreds of lambs in the sunny weather.

Hundreds of dewdrops to greet the dawn,
Hundreds of bees in the purple clover,
Hundreds of butterflies on the lawn,
But only one mother the wide-world over.
—GEORGE COOPER

*L*oving a child doesn't mean giving in to all
his whims; to love him is to bring out the best in
him, to teach him to love what is difficult.
—NADIA BOULANGER

MOTHER-LOVE

The love of a mother is never exhausted.
It never changes, it never tires;
It endures through all; in good repute, in bad repute,
In the face of the world's condemnation,
A mother's love still lives on.
—WASHINGTON IRVING

My education was wholly centered in the glance, more or less serene, and the smile, more or less open, of my mother. The reins of my heart were in her hand. —ALPHONSE DE LAMARTINE

My mother is a poem I'll never be able to write, though everything I write is a poem to my mother. —SHARON DOUBIAGO

MOTHER

There was a place in childhood
That I remember well,
And there a voice of sweetest tone
Bright fairy tales did tell,
And gentle words and fond embrace
Were given with joy to me,
When I was in that happy place
Upon my mother's knee.

—SAMUEL LOVER

A mother isn't paid by the hour or mile; she fills her heart
with a kiss and a smile. —STARLETTE L. HOWARD

*M*other's love grows by giving. —CHARLES LAMB

Mother-love is the fuel that enables a normal human being to do the impossible. —AUTHOR UNKNOWN

THE HAND THAT ROCKS THE CRADLE

They say that man is mighty;
He governs land and sea;
He wields a mighty scepter
O'er lesser powers than he;

But mightier power and stronger
Man from his throne has hurled,
For the hand that rocks the cradle
Is the hand that rules the world.
—WILLIAM ROSS WALLACE

$\mathcal{I}$ drank in, as a plant from the soil, the first nourishing juices of my young intellect from the books carefully selected by my mother. But I drank deep, above all, from my mother's mind.

—ALPHONSE DE LAMARTINE

MOTHER'S LOVE

My mother's love is larkspur, blue and sweet,
The gentle wind along a quiet street.
My mother's love is little silver singing
Of twilight bells, the soft and soundless winging
Of birds in flight across an evening sky,
The first star, hushed and gold and high;
And on all pathways, whether joy or grief,
The clear, unwavering candle of belief.
—GRACE V. WATKINS

Children are likely to live up to what you believe of them. —LADY BIRD JOHNSON

Judicious mothers will always keep in mind that they are the first book read and the last put aside in every child's library. —C. LENOX REMOND

THE READING MOTHER

I had a mother who read to me
Sagas of pirates who scoured the sea,
Cutlasses clenched in their yellow teeth,
"Blackbirds" stowed in the hold beneath.

I had a mother who read me lays
Of ancient and gallant and golden days;
Stories of Marmion and Ivanhoe,
Which every boy has a right to know.

I had a mother who read me tales
   Of Gêlert the hound of the hills of Wales,
   True to his trust till his tragic death,
   Faithfulness blent with his final breath.

I had a mother who read me the things
That wholesome life to the boy-heart brings—
Stories that stir with an upward touch,
Oh, that each mother of boys were such!

You may have tangible wealth untold,
Caskets of jewels and coffers of gold.
Richer than I you can never be—
I had a mother who read to me.
—STRICKLAND GILLIAN

Beauty does not lie in the face. It lies in the harmony between man and his industry. Beauty is expression. When I paint a mother I try to render her beautiful by the mere look she gives her child. —JEAN MILLET

MOTHERS

I think God took the fragrance of a flower,
A pure white flower which blooms not for world praise
But which makes sweet and beautiful some bower;
The compassion of the dew, which gently lays
Reviving freshness on the fainting earth
And gives to all the tired things new birth;
The steadfastness and radiance of stars
Which lift the soul above the confining bar;
The gladness of fair dawns; the sunset's peace;
Contentment which from "trivial rounds" asks no release;
The life which finds its greatest joy in deeds of love for others—
I think God took these precious things and made of them the mothers.
—AUTHOR UNKNOWN

An ounce of mother is worth a pound of clergy. —SPANISH PROVERB

MOTHER'S HANDS

Mother's hands were busy hands
But never did they fail
To take the time to tie a bow
Or braid a loose pigtail.
And never did those hands refuse
To soothe a fevered brow,
So even injured dolls pulled through
In Mother's hands, somehow.

It seemed those hands were magic,
Always knowing where to start
To reconstruct a shattered dream
Or mend a broken heart.
—LOIS J. FUNK

A MOTHER'S LOVE

To mark its growth from day to day,
Its opening charms admire,
Catch from his eye the earliest ray
Of intellectual fire;
To smile and listen while he talks
And lend a finger when he walks;
This is a mother's love.
—JAMES MONTGOMERY

Every mother has the breathtaking
privilege of sharing with God in the
creation of new life. She helps bring
into existence a soul that will endure
for all eternity. —JAMES KELLER

A SONG FOR MY MOTHER—HER STORIES

I always liked to go to bed—
It looked so dear and white.
Besides, my mother used to tell
A story every night.

The room was full of slumber lights,
Of seas and ships and wings,
Of Holy Grails and swords and knights
And beautiful, kind kings.

And so she wove and wove and wove
Her singing thoughts through mine.
I heard them murmuring through my sleep,
Sweet, audible, and fine.

Beneath my pillow all night long
I heard her stories sing,

So spun through the enchanted sheet
Was their soft shadowing.

Dear custom, stronger than the years—
Then let me not grow dull!
Still every night my bed appears
Friendly and beautiful!

Even now when I lie down to sleep,
It comes like a caress;
And still, somehow, my childish heart
Expects a pleasantness.

I find in the remembering sheets
Old stories told by her,
And they are sweet as rosemary
And dim as lavender.

—ANNA HEMPSTEAD BRANCH

$\mathcal{M}$y mother was an angel on earth. She was a minister of blessing to all human beings within her sphere of action. —JOHN QUINCY ADAMS

MOTHER'S GARDEN

In memory I see again a garden I still love,
My mother's flower garden with blue skies up above.

There were pansies with gay colored faces
And honeysuckle sweet by the gate
Through which we children would scamper,
Especially if we were late.

Old-fashioned roses grew in abundance,
Seven-sisters and moss roses too;
I couldn't forget the bachelor buttons,
My favorites were the blue.

There were larkspur and sweet william,
And daisies that grew by the well.

Zinnias, mums, and begonias
Lined a walk made out of crushed shell.

I would not forget the sweet peas,
Nor morning glories twined 'round the door
In my mother's old-fashioned garden,
A garden that grows there no more.

In my memory its fragrance lingers;
Its beauty will always last
As I dream of Mother's garden
And our memories of the past.
—JAYNE D. BURRIER

To talk to a child, to fascinate him, is much more difficult than to
win an electoral victory. But it is more rewarding. —COLETTE

There is no velvet so soft as a mother's lap, no rose so lovely as her smile, no path so flowery as that imprinted with her footsteps.
—ARCHBISHOP THOMSON

A MOTHER'S LOVE

I worship thee, O sun! whose ample light,
Blessing every forehead, ripening every fruit,
Entering every flower and every hovel,
Pours itself forth and yet is never less,
Still spending and unspent—like a mother's love.
—EDMOND ROSTAND

Blessed are the mothers of the earth, for they have combined the practical and the spiritual into one workable way of life. They have darned little stockings, mended little dresses, washed little faces, and pointed little eyes to the stars, and little souls to eternal things. —WILLIAM L. STIDGER

$\mathcal{M}$y mother was the most beautiful woman I ever saw. All I am I owe to my mother. I attribute all my success in life to the moral, intellectual, and physical education I received from her. —GEORGE WASHINGTON

$\mathcal{A}$ mother's kiss made me a painter. —BENJAMIN WEST

$\mathcal{N}$o joy in nature is so sublimely affecting as the joy of a mother at the good fortune of her child. —JEAN PAUL RICHTER

MOTHER'S INFLUENCE

Oh, wondrous power! How little understood,
Entrusted to the mother's mind alone
To fashion genius, form the soul for good,
Inspire a West, or train a Washington.

—SARAH HALE

THIRTY

If you would reform the
world from its errors and vices,
begin by enlisting the mothers.
—C. Simmons

MY MOTHER

She was as good as goodness is;
Her acts and all her words were kind,
And high above all memories
I hold the beauty of her mind.
—Frederic H. Adams

MY TRUST

A picture memory brings to me:
I look across the years and see
Myself beside my mother's knee.
I feel her gentle hand restrain
My selfish moods and know again
A child's blind sense of wrong and pain.

But wiser now, a man gray grown,
My childhood's needs are better known,
My mother's chastening love I own.
—John Greenleaf Whittier

Some are kissing mothers and some are scolding mothers; but it is love just
the same, and most mothers kiss and scold together. —Pearl S. Buck

OUR MOTHER

Our mother bade us keep the trodden ways,
Stroked down my tippet, set my brother's frill,
Then with the benediction of her gaze,
Clung to us lessening and pursued us still
Across the homestead to the rookery elms
Whose tall old trunks had each a grassy mound
So rich for us we counted them as realms
With varied products; here were earth nuts found
And here the ladyfingers, in deep shade,
Here sloping toward the moat, the rushes grew,
The large to split for pith, the small to braid,
While over all the dark rooks cawing flew . . .
And made a happy strange solemnity
A deep-toned chant from life unknown to me.

—GEORGE ELIOT

Mama exhorted her children at every opportunity to "jump at de sun." We might not land on the sun, but at least we would get off the ground. —ZORA NEALE HURSTON

SHE WORKS AT TASKS

She works at tasks
Requiring no especial skill,
Yet making their demands,
Hard to fulfill,
Demand on time and patience
And the capricious will.

Grease blears the gaze
Of water cooling in the bowl
And films her wrists and hands;

Toil takes its toll
Of strength, drains light and music
From the air and numbs the soul;

Or surely would
Except her love re-makes all things,
And every trivial chore,
Transmuted, brings
A sacramental joy
And, while she works, she sings.
—VERNON SCANNELL

*A*fter more than twenty years of parenting, I have come to the conclusion that being a mother is just as much about being a learner. Sometimes the lessons are difficult, sometimes they are frustrating, at times they are downright frightening and, on occasion, even hilarious. I am still a mother, and therefore still a learner, taught by some of the most ingenious instructors I know—my children. —PAMELA KENNEDY

THE ADVERSARY

A mother's hardest to forgive.
Life is the fruit she longs to hand you,
Ripe on a plate. And while you live,
Relentlessly she understands you.
—PHYLLIS McGINLEY

IN AN IRIDESCENT TIME

My mother when young, scrubbed laundry in a tub,
She and her sisters on an old brick walk
Under the apple trees, sweet rub-a-dub.
The bees came round their heads; the wrens made talk.
Four young ladies, each with a rainbow board,
Honed their knuckles, wrung their wrists to red,
Tossed back their braids, and wiped their aprons wet.
The Jersey calf beyond the back fence roared;
And all the soft day, swarms about their pet
Buzzed at his big brown eyes and bullish head.
Four times they rinsed, they said. Some things they starched,
Then shot them from the baskets two by two,
And pinned the fluttering intimacies of life
Between the lilac bushes and the yew:
Brown gingham, pink, and skirts of Alice blue.
—RUTH STONE

MOMMA

Momma
pale as the Southern secrets
in her blood
was princess of morning.

She rose alone
to apocalyptic silence,
set the sun in our windows
and daily mended the world

through years of never-enough,
hiding her dreams
in a typewriter
rusting beneath the kitchen sink.

In weary dresses
that would not survive the Fifties
she gifted us with memory
and created home.
—PAULETTE CHILDRESS WHITE

The future destiny of the child is always in the work of the mother.
—NAPOLEON BONAPARTE

Time or circumstance may come between a mother and her
child; however, their lives are interwoven forever. —PAM BROWN

For when you look into my mother's eyes, you knew, as if He had told you, why God sent her into the world—it was to open the minds, of all who looked, to beautiful thoughts. —JAMES M. BARRIE

MY MAMA MOVED AMONG THE DAYS

My Mama moved among the days
like a dream-walker in a field;
seemed like what she touched was hers
seemed like what touched her couldn't hold,
she got us almost through the high grass
then seemed like she turned around and ran
right back in
right back on in.
—LUCILLE CLIFTON

The mother's heart is the child's schoolroom. —HENRY WARD BEECHER

Mothering should involve both taking care of someone who
is dependent and at the same time supporting that person in his
or her efforts to become independent. —SIGNE HAMMER

MOTHER, IN SUNLIGHT

I tugged at your skirt, and you smiled.

You stood in sunlight
Near the coal stove
A black iron heating,
A black iron slicking wrinkles
On percale dresses and starched white shirts.
Sweat dripping down your brow.

I think of the hours you spent
To make our world sparkle.
—LOUISE ROBINSON-BOARDLEY

The phrase "working mother" is redundant.
—JANE SELLMAN

A mother doesn't walk, but runs, to smooth the human pathway she knows her child must tread. —JEANNE HILL

Sometimes the strength of motherhood is greater than natural laws.

—BARBARA KINGSOLVER

TO MY MOTHER

Because the angels in the heavens above,
Devoutly singing unto one another,
Can find amid their burning terms of love
None so devotional as that of "Mother,"
Therefore by that sweet name I long have called you;
You who are more than mother unto me,
Filling my heart of hearts, where God installed you,
In setting my Virginia's spirit free.
My mother—my own mother, who died early,
Was but the mother of myself; but you
Are mother to the dead I loved so dearly,
Are thus more precious than the one I knew,
By that infinity with which my wife
Was dearer to my soul than its soul life.

—EDGAR ALLAN POE

TRIBUTE TO A MOTHER

Faith that withstood the shocks of toil and time;
Hope that defied despair;
Patience that conquered care;
And loyalty, whose courage was sublime;
The great deep heart that was a home for all—
Just, eloquent, and strong
In protest against wrong;
Wide charity that knew no sin, no fall;
The Spartan spirit that made life so grand,
Mating poor daily needs
With high, heroic deeds,
That wrested happiness from Fate's hard hand.
—LOUISA MAY ALCOTT

In search of my mother's garden, I found my own. —ALICE WALKER

THE MOTHER OF A POET

She is too kind, I think, for mortal things,
Too gentle for the gusty ways of earth;
God gave to her a shy and silver mirth
And made her soul as clear
And softly singing as an orchard spring's
In sheltered hollows all the sunny year—
A spring that through the leaning grass looks up
And holds all heaven in its clear cup,
Mirror to holy meadows high and blue
With stars like drops of dew.
—SARA TEASDALE

The worst to be said about mothers is that they are prone to give kisses of congratulations which make you feel like a battleship on which someone is breaking a bottle. —NORMAN MAILER

TO MY MOTHER

In childhood days, dear Mother, it was you
Who taught me all of nature's loveliness.
How, from the sodden leaf mold, violets grew
To fragrant beauty 'neath the sun's caress.
You pointed out the tender, living green
Of lichen growing on the rocky ledge;
The mullein stalk, like plush; the mellow sheen
Of bittersweet, twined on the frosted hedge.
You taught the gracefulness of leafless trees
(The twigs wove tapestry against the sky),
And in the thaw-wet furrows, even these
Would bear the gold of harvest by and by.

And I, in wood, in field, in bare brown sod,
Found everywhere the hidden touch of God.
—MAY ALLREAD BAKER

There is an enduring tenderness in the love of a mother to a son that transcends all other affections of the heart. —WASHINGTON IRVING

TO MY MOTHER

My heart's devotion do I bring thee, Mother dear;
For more and more I realize each passing year
What thy great love and care has always meant to me.
And what a debt of fealty I owe to thee:
My advent into life was through thy mortal pain,
And in my careless childhood days thou dids't refrain
From many pleasures that might otherwise be thine
In order to direct those restless feet of mine.
—LEROY HURON KELSEY

My first desire for knowledge and my earliest passion for reading were awakened by my mother. —CHARLES DICKENS

TO MOTHER

Sonnets are full of love, and this my tome
Has many sonnets: so here now, shall be
One sonnet more, a love sonnet, from me
To her whose heart is my heart's quiet home,
To my first love, my Mother, on whose knee
I learnt love-lore that is not troublesome;
Whose service is my special dignity,
And she my lodestar while I go and come.
And so because you love me and because
I love you, Mother, I have woven a wreath
Of rhymes wherewith to crown your honored name:
In you not fourscore years can dim the flame
Of love, whose blessed glow transcends the laws
Of time and change and mortal life and death.
—CHRISTINA G. ROSSETTI

*G*od shows that He
is everywhere by the
triumph and power
of a mother's love.
—AUTHOR UNKNOWN

When you are a mother, you are never really alone in your thoughts. You are connected to your child and to all those who touch your lives. A mother always has to think twice, once for herself and once for her child. —SOPHIA LOREN

MOTHER'S TEA SET

Around these entwined and faded
Roses, the jam pots, the smell
Of baking, the lidless sugar bowl,
And the amber stained pot,
You opened your woman's world
To me: how good friends
Are as necessary as air;
How to hold my chin up and push
The world away with one

Deep breath; how to knead
Biscuit dough only ten times,
More makes them tough; and
That men need strong women
And strong coffee. Layer by layer,
Cup by cup, my role, your life,
Was revealed.

Your chipped cups still hold
The sweetness of my world.

—ANNE NORMAN

*S*tories first heard at a mother's knee are never wholly forgotten—
a little spring that never quite dries up in our journey through
scorching years. —RUFFINI

$\mathcal{M}$ighty is the force of motherhood! It transforms all things by its vital heart; it turns timidity into fierce courage, and dreadless defiance into tremulous submission; it turns thoughtlessness into foresight, and yet stills all self-denial into calm content. —GEORGE ELIOT

ALL PATHS LEAD TO YOU

All paths lead to you
　　Where e'er I stray;
You are the evening star at the end of the day.
All paths lead to you,
　　Hill-top or low;
You are the white birch in the sun's glow.
All paths lead to you
　　Where e'er I roam;
You are the lark-song calling me home.
—BLANCHE SHOEMAKER WAGSTAFF

PIANO

Softly, in the dusk, a woman is singing to me;
Taking me back down the vista of years, till I see
A child sitting under the piano, in the boom of the tingling strings
And pressing the small, poised feet of a mother who smiles as she sings.

In spite of myself, the insidious mastery of song
Betrays me back, till the heart of me weeps to belong
To the old Sunday evenings at home with winter outside
And hymns in the cosy parlour, the tinkling piano our guide.

So now it is vain for the singer to burst into clamour
With the great black piano appassionato. The glamour
Of childish days is upon me, my manhood is cast
Down in the flood of remembrance, I weep like a child for the past.

—D. H. LAWRENCE

CHILD OF THE SEASIDE

My mother grew to girlhood
Between the sea and pines
Where to guide the schooners
A golden beacon shines.
Something there was in her
Kin to the stalwart soul
Of pines that bow to tempests
And rise unhurt and whole.

And of the sea's bright laughter
She was formed in part,
Sunlight on dimpling water
Lingered in her heart.
And like the spark that guided
The little boats to shore
Drifting voyagers steered by
The light her spirit wore.

—MARY B. WALL

My mother and I have a special relationship. We have an
agreement that I can tell her my problems as I would tell a friend,
and she will give advice from a friend's standpoint. . . .
I admire my mother more than anyone in the world.

—LYNDA BIRD ROBB

FIFTY-TWO

TO MOTHER

You painted no Madonnas
On chapel walls in Rome,
But with a touch diviner
You lived one in your home.

You wrote no lofty poems
That critics counted art,
But with a nobler vision
You lived them in your heart.

You carved no shapeless marble
To some high soul design,
But with a finer sculpture
You shaped this soul of mine.

You built no great cathedrals
That centuries applaud,
But with a grace exquisite
Your life cathedraled God.

Had I the gift of Raphael,
Or Michelangelo,
Oh, what a rare Madonna
My mother's life would show.

—WILLIAM PITT FESSENDEN

There is so much to teach, and the time goes so fast. —ERMA BOMBECK

CAUGHT

There is in the human voice
A quavery vowel sometimes,
More animal than meaning,
More mineral than gentle,

A slight nuance by which my
Mother would recognize lies,
Detect scorn, or envy, sober
Things words would not admit,

Though it's true the best liars
Must never know they lie.
They move among good-byes
Worded like congratulations

We listen for and hear until
Some misery draws us back
To what it really was they
Obviously meant not to say.

And misery often draws us
Out to meadows or trees,
That speechless life where
Everything inhuman is true.

Mother spoke for tentative
People, illiterate, unsure.
Thinking of it her way is to
Reduce all words to tones

The wind might make anytime
With a few dead leaves. Our
Own names called in the dark
Or quail rising. Sounds that

Go straight from the ear to
The heart. There all the time,
They are a surface too clear
To see. Written down, no

Matter how right, they are too
Slow and vain as those soft
Vows we spoke in childhood to
Wild things, birds, or rabbits

We meant to charm. When
My mother mentioned oaks,
They could be cut down, sawn
Into boards and nailed together

As rooms, and she was mostly
Quiet, standing in the kitchen,
Her pin rolling like law
Across plains of biscuit dough

While dark ripened, wind
Died on the tongue of each leaf.
The night broke in pieces
If she cleared her throat.

—RODNEY JONES

TO A MOTHER

Know, I am never far from you; I bear you
Inwardly as you bore me—as intimately too,
And as my flesh is of your own
And our early mesh woven one,
So you are still my own;
And everything about you, home,
The features, eyes, the hands, your entire form
Are the past, present, and to come,
The familiarity, the ease
Of my living, and my peace.
—SISTER MARY AGNES

When I stopped seeing my mother with the eyes of a child, I saw
the woman who helped me give birth to myself. —NANCY FRIDAY

MY MOTHER

I walk upon the rocky shore,
Her strength is in the ocean's roar.
I glance into the shaded pool,
Her mind is there so calm and cool.
I hear sweet rippling of the sea,
Naught but her laughter 'tis to me.

I gaze into the starry skies,
And there I see her wondrous eyes.
I look into my inmost mind,
And here her inspiration find.
In all I am and hear and see,
My precious mother is with me.

—JOSEPHINE RICE CREELMAN

Countless times each day a mother does what no one else can do quite as well. She wipes away a tear, whispers a word of hope, eases a child's fear. She teaches, ministers, loves, and nurtures the next generation of citizens. And she challenges and cajoles her kids to do their best and be their best. —JAMES DOBSON AND GARY L. BAUER

A VALENTINE TO MY MOTHER

My blessed Mother, dozing in her chair
On Christmas Day, seemed an embodied Love,
A comfortable Love with soft brown hair
Softened and silvered to a tint of dove;
A better sort of Venus with an air
Angelical from thoughts that dwell above;
A wiser Pallas in whose body fair
Enshrined a blessed soul looks out thereof.
Winter brought holly then; now spring has brought
Paler and frailer snowdrops shivering;
And I have brought a simple humble thought—
I, her devoted duteous Valentine—
A lifelong thought which drills this song I sing,
A lifelong love to this dear saint of mine.

—CHRISTINA G. ROSSETTI

A mother's arms are made of tenderness, and children sleep soundly in them.

—VICTOR HUGO

The world tips away when we look in our children's faces. —LOUISE ERDRICH

*G*od gives us friends, and that means much; but far
above all others, the richest of His gifts to earth was
when He thought of mothers. —AUTHOR UNKNOWN

THE CHAIR IN WHICH YOU'VE SAT

The chair in which you've sat's not just a chair
nor the table at which you've eaten just a table
nor the window that you've looked from just a window.
All these have now a patina of your
body and mind, a kind of ghostly glow which
haloes them a little, though invisible.
—IAIN CHRICHTON SMITH

The mother is a gardener—planting the seeds of faith, truth, and
love that develop into the fairest flowers of her character: virtue
and happiness in the lives of her children. —J. HAROLD GWYNNE

The commonest fallacy among women is that simply having children
makes one a mother—which is almost as absurd as believing that having
a piano makes one a musician. —SYDNEY J. HARRIS

TO MOTHER

You are the golden link between the days
Of happy, careless childhood and this hour.
Because of you I know green and woodland ways,
And quaint old country gardens burst in flower.
There will be meadowlands where children run
And daisies lift shy faces to the blue;
There will be brooks that sparkle in the sun
As long as I have you!
—ANNE CAMPBELL

She never outgrows the burden of love, and to the end she carries the
weight of hope for those she bore. —FLORIDA SCOTT-MAXWELL

And wherever we may turn, this lesson we shall learn:
a boy's best friend is his mother. —JOSEPH P. SKELLEY

MY MOTHER'S GARDEN

Her heart is like her garden,
Old-fashioned, quaint, and sweet,
With here a wealth of blossoms
And there a still retreat.
Sweet violets are hiding,
We know as we pass by,
And lilies, pure as angel thoughts,
Are opening somewhere nigh.

Forget-me-nots there linger,
To full perfection brought,
And there bloom purple pansies
In many a tender thought.

There love's own roses blossom,
As from enchanted ground,
And lavish perfume exquisite
The whole glad year around.

And in the quiet garden—
The garden of her heart—
Songbirds are always singing
Their songs of cheer apart.
And from it floats forever,
O'ercoming sin and strife,
Sweet as the breath of roses blown,
The fragrance of her life.

—ALICE E. ALLEN

Home is the one place in all this world where hearts are sure of each other. It is the place of confidence. —FREDERICK W. ROBERTSON

TO MY MOTHER

I've gone about for years, I find,
With eyes half blind,
Squandering golden hours
In search of flowers
That do not grow, it seems,
Except in dreams;
But in my wanderings
From place to place
I've found more fair no face—
No eyes more true than thine,
O Mother mine.
—EDWARD SALISBURY FIELD

A mother's love! If there be one thing pure where all beside is sullied, that can endure when all else passes away, if there be aught surpassing human deed or word or thought, it is a mother's love.
—MARCHIONESS DE SPADARA

A man never sees all that his mother has been to him till it's too late to let her know that he sees it. —WILLIAM DEAN HOWELLS

TO MY MOTHER—A TRUE GARDENER

To you who've lived your life elate
In Marvell's happy garden state,
And doubtless see, with Milton's eyes,
Eden a flow'ry paradise,
While every walk that you have trod,
Was Enoch's walk, a walk with God—

To you this little book I bring
Wherein our English poets sing
Of all the pleasures they have found
In gardens grayly walled around,
Of tranquil toil and studious ease,
Mid flowers, shrubberies, and trees,
Because you Cowley's wish have known
To have a garden of your own,

And having it, have plied that art
Which Temple calls the ladies' part
So well, your skill might seem to be
A kind of gentle wizardry;
As still your flowers statelier grow
And with a richer color glow
Each summer, and perfume the air
More sweetly from each gay parterre.

Ah, I recall the city plot
That was your scanty garden spot
In other years, and yet your care
Made e'en those narrow beds to bear
The narrower flinty walks between,
Such wealth of red and white and green

That prouder gardens might have sighted,
Grown pale through envy, and so, died.

But now you hold your gentle sway
O'er a domain as broad as they,
Where you may tend with tranquil mind
The seeds and shoots and bulbs consigned
Each season to the garden soil;

Till, reared by you with patient toil,
At length in flaunting rows they stand
And keep the order you have planned,
The low before, the tall behind,
Their colors mingled and combined,
Gay household troops in order drawn
As for review upon the lawn,
While you the colonel seem to me
Of summer's splendid soldiery.
—WILLIAM ASPENWALL BRADLEY

My mother was the making of me. She was so true,
so sure of me, and I felt that I had someone to live for,
someone I must not disappoint. —THOMAS EDISON

SIXTY-SIX

THE WATCHER

She always leaned to watch for us,
Anxious if we were late,
In the winter by the window,
In the summer by the gate.

And though we mocked her tenderly,
Who had such foolish care,
The long way home would seem more safe
Because she waited there.
—MARGARET WIDDEMER

A mother is not a person
to lean on but a person to
make leaning unnecessary.
—DOROTHY CANFIELD FISHER

*A*ll my life I never really thought of her as Mother in the
sense that some people think of a parent. I thought of her more
as a great woman. —PEARL BAILEY

FROM TWO MOMENTS, FOR MY MOTHER

The nights I don't sleep, like the days I sleepwalk through—

I am thinking about your hand on my forehead,
how it let the pain shine, go dark, and cool,

how you sat there, hours, talking, saying my name,
telling the story of the new moon.

What you called a coal-star, red ash soft in the wind,
still blows down on the lawn. A sign, you said.

And who can sleep whose bed is not by the window?
The sky in the maple still turns and turns and lets the wind

in first, then rain, then a light that is nothing
but silver off the leaves.

I am alive because of you.
I am alive all night, and in the morning,
like a penny's worth of fever, the sun is alive,

one color, then another—lily, chrysanthemum, dew.
—STANLEY PLUMLY

Men are what their mothers make them. —RALPH WALDO EMERSON

No man can ever appreciate the debt he owes his mother,
but sometimes a little thing may come up to set him thinking.
—EDWIN ARLINGTON ROBINSON

Happy is he with such a mother! —ALFRED, LORD TENNYSON

IF THERE ARE ANY HEAVENS MY
MOTHER WILL(ALL BY HERSELF)HAVE

if there are any heavens my mother will(all by herself)have
one. It will not be a pansy heaven nor
a fragile heaven of lilies-of-the-valley but
it will be a heaven of blackred roses

my father will be(deep like a rose
tall like a rose)

standing near my

swaying over her
(silent)
with eyes which are really petals and see

nothing with the face of a poet really which

is a flower and not a face with
hands
which whisper
This is my beloved my

    (suddenly in sunlight

he will bow,

& the whole garden will bow)
—E. E. CUMMINGS

Men and women
frequently forget each
other, but everybody
remembers mother.
—JEROME PAINE BATES

My mama was really alert. She seemed to know every second
where I was, what I was up to, and who I was with. She had a seventh
sense and seemed to know if I was just planning to do something that
was out of order. —PAT BOONE

*A*ll mothers are rich when they love their children. There are no poor mothers, no ugly ones, no old ones. Their love is always the most beautiful of the joys. And when they seem most sad, it needs but a kiss which they receive or give to turn all their tears into stars. —MAURICE MAETERLINCK

MOTHER

Never thought for self had she.
Never for herself ambition.
Goal of all her dreams were we,
Holding us her earthly mission.

We were first in every thought.
Friend or foe could not divert her.
Failing her in what she taught,
We alone had power to hurt her.

Looking back, we know today
We were source of all her gladness,
And whene'er we went astray
We were source of all her sadness.

This the mother that we knew!
Never any life was purer.
Gentle, tender, brave and true,
Never any love was surer!

—EDGAR GUEST

Let parents bequeath to their children not
riches, but the spirit of reverence. —PLATO

No man is poor who has had a godly mother. —ABRAHAM LINCOLN

No gift to your mother can ever equal her gift to you—
life. —AUTHOR UNKNOWN

A MOTHER'S ROLE

Her office then to rear, to teach,
Becoming as is meet and fit,
A link among the days, to knit
The generations each with each.
—ALFRED, LORD TENNYSON

It will be gone before you know it. The fingerprints on the wall appear
higher and higher. Then suddenly they disappear. —DOROTHY EVSLIN

Her children arise up and call her blessed. —PROVERBS 31:28

MOTHER AND I

O Mother, my love, if you'll give me your hand
And go where I ask you to wander,
I will lead you away to this beautiful land—
The dreamland that's waiting out yonder.
We'll walk in a sweet posy garden out there,
Where moonlight and starlight are streaming,
And the flowers and the birds are filling the air
With the fragrance and music of dreaming.
There'll be no little tired-out boy to undress,
No questions or cares to perplex you;
There'll be no little bruises or bumps to caress,
Nor patching of socks to vex you.
For I'll rock you away on a silver-dew stream
And sing you asleep when you're weary,
And no one shall know of our beautiful dream
But you and your own little dearie.

—EUGENE FIELD

FROM DUET FOR ONE VOICE

We escape from our mothers
again and again, young
Houdinis playing the usual matinees.
First comes escape down
the birth canal, our newly carved faces
leading the way like figureheads
on ancient slaveships,
our small hands rowing for life.
Later escape into silence, escape
behind slammed doors,
the flight into marriage.
I thought I was finally old enough
to sit with you, sharing a book.
But when I look up from the page, you
have escaped from me.

—LINDA PASTAN

A CHILD'S SONG TO HER MOTHER

The lovely years went lightly by
As April flowers go,
And often you would laugh or cry
To see how I could grow.
The lonely years drift by in rain,
As leaves in autumn do.
I long, when we shall meet again,
To be as tall as you.

—WINIFRED WELLES

A mother's love has all the stars of heaven shining down on it at night.

—CATHERINE BEECHER

A mother's love is indeed the golden link that binds youth to age; and he is still but a child, however time may have furrowed his cheek or silvered his brow, who can yet recall, with a softened heart, the fond devotion or the gentle chidings of the best friend that God ever gives us. —C. NESTELL BOVÉE

TO MOTHER

I hope that soon, dear Mother,
You and I may be
In the quiet room my fancy
Has so often made for thee—

The pleasant, sunny chamber;
The cushioned easy-chair;
The book laid for your reading;
The vase of flowers fair;

The desk beside the window
Where the sun shines warm and bright,
And there in ease and quiet
The promised book you write,

While I sit close beside you,
Content at last to see
That you can rest, dear Mother,
And I can cherish thee.

—LOUISA MAY ALCOTT

You may have friends—fond, dear friends—but never will you have again the inexpressible love and gentleness lavished upon you which none but a mother bestows.

—THOMAS BABINGTON MACAULAY

Mother is indeed a sweet name, and her station is indeed a holy one; for in her hands are placed minds to be molded almost at her will. —AUTHOR UNKNOWN

MY MOTHER'S HANDS

Such beautiful, beautiful hands,
They're neither white nor small;
And you, I know, would scarcely think
That they were fair at all.

I've looked on hands whose form and hue
A sculptor's dream might be,
Yet are these aged wrinkled hands
Most beautiful to me.
—ELLEN M. H. GATES

THE SONG OF THE OLD MOTHER

I rise in the dawn, and I kneel and blow
Till the seed of the fire flicker and glow;
And then I must scrub and bake and sweep
Till stars are beginning to blink and peep;

And the young lie long and dream in their bed
Of the matching of ribbons for bosom and head,
And their day goes over in idleness,
And they sigh if the wind but lift a tress:

While I must work because I am old
And the seed of the fire gets feeble and cold.
　　—WILLIAM BUTLER YEATS

No matter how old a mother is, she watches her middle-aged children for signs of improvement. —FLORIDA SCOTT-MAXWELL

OLD MOTHERS

I love old mothers—mothers with white hair
And kindly eyes, and lips grown softly sweet
With murmured blessings over sleeping babes,
There is a something in their quiet grace
That speaks the calm of Sabbath afternoons;
A knowledge in their deep, unfaltering eyes
That far outreaches all philosophy.

Time, with caressing touch about them, weaves
The silver-threaded fairy-shawl of age,
While all the echoes of forgotten songs
Seem joined to lend a sweetness to their speech.
Old mothers—as they pass with slow-timed step,
Their trembling hands cling gently to youth's strength.
  Sweet mothers—as they pass, one sees again
    Old garden walks, old roses, and old loves.
      —CHARLES SARSFIELD ROSS

A mother's heart, like primroses, opens most beautifully in the evening of life. —AUTHOR UNKNOWN

*B*ecause she is my mother, I so well understand why flowers bloom beneath the touch of her gentle hand. —MARY RITA HURLEY

MOTHER MACHREE

Sure I love the dear silver that shines in your hair,
And the brow that's all furrowed and wrinkled with care.
I kiss the dear fingers, so toil-worn for me,
Oh, God bless you and keep you, Mother Machree.
—RIDA JOHNSON YOUNG

BIOGRAPHIES

of selected poets

LOUISA MAY ALCOTT (1832–1888) American author, poet, teacher, nurse, and editor. Author of *Little Women*.

WILLIAM CULLEN BRYANT (1794–1878) American poet, critic, and editor born in Cummington, Massachusetts. Editor of *New York Evening Post*.

ELIZABETH BARRETT BROWNING (1806–1861) English poet. Lived in Italy with her husband, Robert Browning.

LUCILLE CLIFTON (1936–) American poet, author, and writer of children's books born in Depew, New York. Distinguished Professor of Humanities at St. Mary's College in Maryland.

E. E. CUMMINGS (1894–1962) American poet, critic, painter, and novelist born in Cambridge, Massachusetts. Known for his eccentric use of typography, slang, and punctuation.

GEORGE ELIOT (1819–1880) pseudonym of Mary Ann Evans, English author and poet born in Arbury, Warwickshire. Author of *Middlemarch* and *The Mill on the Floss*.

WILLIAM PITT FESSENDEN (1806–1869) American lawyer, congressman, and financier born in Bocawen, New Hampshire.

EUGENE FIELD (1850–1895) American poet and journalist born in St. Louis, Missouri. Best known for his children's verse.

DOROTHY CANFIELD FISHER (1879–1958) American novelist, short-story writer, and critic born in Kansas. Wrote *The Bent Twig*.

EDGAR GUEST (1881–1959) American poet born in Birmingham, England. Known as "The Poet of the People."

SARAH HALE (1788–1879) American poet and author of children's literature born in New Hampshire. Author of "Mary's Lamb."

DUBOSE HEYWARD (1885–1940) American novelist, poet, and dramatist. Author of *Porgy*, the basis of the Gershwin opera *Porgy and Bess*.

WASHINGTON IRVING (1783–1859) American author and essayist born in New York City. Author of *The Legend of Sleepy Hollow*.

D. H. Lawrence (1885–1930) English author, poet, and essayist born in Nottingham. Author of *Women in Love*, *Lady Chatterley's Lover*, and *Sons and Lovers*.

Samuel Lover (1797–1868) Irish author, artist, and songwriter born in Dublin.

Phyllis McGinley (1905–1977) American humorist and poet. Wrote numerous children's books and essays.

Anne Norman (1968–) American poet born in Richmond, Virginia.

Kathleen Norris (1880–1966) American author born in San Francisco, California. Author of *The Sea Gull* and *My California*.

Edgar Allan Poe (1809–1849) American critic, author, and poet born in Boston, Massachusetts. Author of *The Pit and the Pendulum* and "The Raven."

Christina G. Rossetti (1830–1894) English poet born in London. Devoted the majority of her life to religious study. Author of *Goblin Market and Other Poems*.

Edmond Rostand (1868–1918) French playwright. Author of *Cyrano de Bergerac*.

Robert Louis Stevenson (1850–1894) Scottish author, poet, and essayist. Best known for his children's literature and poetry.

Sara Teasdale (1884–1933) American poet. Awarded a special Pulitzer Prize for *Love Songs*.

Alfred, Lord Tennyson (1809–1892) English poet of Victorian verse. Appointed Poet Laureate in 1850.

William Ross Wallace (1819–1881) American poet and author of lyrical verse and patriotic songs.

John Greenleaf Whittier (1807–1892) American abolitionist, editor, and poet born in Haverhill, Massachusetts.

Margaret Widdemer (1890–1978) American poet and author born in Doylestown, Pennsylvania. Awarded a special Pulitzer Prize in 1918.

William Butler Yeats (1865–1939) Irish writer, nationalist, and poet. Elected senator of the Irish Free State in 1922 and awarded the Nobel Prize in Literature in 1923.

INDEX BY AUTHOR

INDEX BY TITLE

ACKNOWLEDGMENTS (continued from page 4)

LAWRENCE, D. H. "Piano", from THE COMPLETE POEMS OF D. H. LAWRENCE by D. H. Lawrence, edited by V. de Sola Pinto & F. W. Roberts, copyright © 1964, 1971 by Angelo Ravagli and C. M. Weekley, Executors of the Estate of Frieda Lawrence Ravagli. Used by permission of Viking Penguin, a division of Penguin Putnam Inc. McGINLEY, PHYLLIS. "The Adversary", copyright © 1959 by Phyllis McGinley, from TIMES THREE by Phyllis McGinley. Used by permission of Viking Penguin, a division of Penguin Putnam Inc. PASTAN, LINDA. Excerpt from "Duet for One Voice", from A FRACTION OF DARKNESS by Linda Pastan. Copyright © 1985 by Linda Pastan. Reprinted by permission of W. W. Norton & Company, Inc. PLUMLY, STANLEY. Excerpt from "Two Moments, for My Mother" from SUMMER CELESTIAL by Stanley Plumly. Reprinted by permission of the author. SCANNELL, VERNON. "She Works at Tasks" from THE LOVING GAME by Vernon Scannell. Reprinted by permission of the publisher, Robson Books, Ltd. SMITH, IAIN CRICHTON. "The Chair in Which You've Sat" from LOVE POEMS AND ELEGIES by Iain Crichton Smith. Reprinted by permission of the publishers, Victor Gollancz. STONE, RUTH. "In an Iridescent Time." Used by permission of the author. WHITE, PAULETTE CHILDRESS. "Momma." Reprinted by permission of the author. YEATS, W. B. "The Song of the Old Mother." Reprinted with the permission of Simon & Schuster from THE POEMS OF W. B. YEATS: A NEW EDTION, edited by Richard J. Finneran. Copyright 1933 by Macmillan Publishing Company; copyright renewed © 1961 by Bertha Georgie Yeats. Our sincere thanks to the following authors whom we were unable to locate: Alice E. Allen for "My Mother's Garden," May All-read Baker for "To My Mother," Anna Hempstead Branch for "Songs for My Mother—Her Stories," Anne Campbell for "To Mother," Strickland Gillian for "The Reading Mother," Louise Robinson-Boardley for "Mother, in Sunlight," Grace V. Watkins for "Mother's Love."